Good Morning Hope

By Heather Martin

ACKNOWLEDGEMENTS

Cover design: Jacob Martin

Inside design: Lorinda Gray/Ragamuffin Creative

Editing: Carol Guess

Copyright 2016 by Heather Martin

All rights reserved. This book is protected by the copyright laws of the United States of America. This book may not be copied or reprinted for commercial gain or profit. The use of short quotations or occasional page copying for personal or group study is permitted and encouraged. Unless otherwise identified, Scripture quotations are from the New International Version. Copyright 1982 by Thomas Nelson, Inc. Used by Permission. Scripture quotations from THE MESSAGE. Copyright by Eugene Peterson 1993, 1994, 1995, 1996, 2000, 2001, 2002. Used by permission of NavPress. All rights reserved. Represented by Tyndall House Publishers, INC. Please note that the author's publishing style capitalizes certain pronouns in Scripture that refer to the Father, Son and Holy Spirit, and may differ from other publisher's styles.

ISBN: 978-0-692-74888-6

Printed in the U.S.A.

DEDICATION

This book is dedicated to my tribe:

Jacob, Morgan, Madison, Judah, and Jonathan.

My family is my greatest accomplishment and gift, this side of Heaven.

Jacob, you challenge me with such tenderness and love, you're my best friend and I love you more than words.

To my children
(Morgan, Madison, Judah, and Jonathan),
you make being a mother a joy.
I am so proud of all of you.

TABLE OF CONTENTS

Day 1	Faith	1
Day 2	Connected	3
Day 3	Thankful	5
Day 4	Growth	7
Day 5	Courage	9
Day 6	Comfort	11
Day 7	Self-Control	13
Day 8	Trust	15
Day 9	Trials	17
Day 10	Freedom	19
Day 11	Peace	21
Day 12	Joy	23
Day 13	Restless	25
Day 14	Disciple	27
Day 15	Selfless	29

Day 16	Dance	31
Day 17	Generous	33
Day 18	Fear	35
Day 19	Love	37
Day 20	Power	39
Day 21	Future	41
Day 22	Redemption	43
Day 23	Righteousness	45
Day 24	Sleep	47
Day 25	Deliverance	49
Day 26	Prosperity	51
Day 27	Prayer	53
Day 28	Voice	55
Day 29	Shame	57
Day 30	Honor	59

FAITH

... AS JESUS WENT ON FROM THERE, two blind men followed him, calling out, "Have mercy on us, Son of David!" When he had gone indoors, the blind men came to him, and he asked them, "Do you believe that I am able to do this?" "Yes, Lord," they replied. Then he touched their eyes and said, "According to your FAITH will it be done to you," and their sight was restored. (Matthew 9:27-30 NIV)

According to your faith... if your faith was a gasoline tank, how full or empty would it be? Could you make a cross country trip on your faith tank or just a quick trip to the grocery store? A challenge is presented to us from Jesus — According to YOUR faith. Faith expects from God what is impossible from man. Faith is confidence in what we hope for, assurance about what we don't yet see (Hebrews 11:1).

God wants you to dream BIG, full of faith that He is a faithful father that knows how to give good gifts to His children. He wants you to have a vision for your future and the faith that He will help you get there.

Without faith you cannot please God and get to where He's calling you to go. By faith you partner with God and your gasoline tank is always full and ready to go anywhere at anytime.

DECLARE: My faith tank if being filled to overflow. As I partner with God, by faith, He speaks to me and shows me the best way to go. My faith produces fruit for the Kingdom of Heaven changing me and my family. I am excited about my faith journey!

NOTES

CONNECTED

LET US DRAW NEAR TO GOD with a sincere heart in full assurance of faith, having our hearts sprinkled to cleanse us from a guilty conscience and having our bodies washed with pure water. Let us hold unswervingly to the hope we profess, for he who promised is faithful. And let us consider how we may spur one another on toward love and good deeds. Let us not give up meeting together, as some are in the habit of doing, but let us encourage one another - and all the more as you see the day approaching. (Hebrews 10:22-25 NIV)

We have drawn near to a loving Father who has cleansed us from our guilty conscience and made us clean. We are clean. We have hope in what the future holds. The future holds a challenge to stay connected to a body of believers and encourage each other with the gifts God deposited inside us.

If meeting together was important to Jesus and his disciples and the early church, than the same should be true for us today! We must place a priority on staying connected to the community God has placed us in. Too many times we let excuses rob us from the opportunity to be encouraged and to use the gifts that are burning on the inside of us. Our gifts were given to us for the purpose of staying connected to community. As we faithfully steward those gifts, God blesses the work of our hands and the Kingdom of Heaven is expanded.

DECLARE: Being connected to my church community is a priority in my life. As I stay connected, my gifts grow and I see the fruit for which I have prayed. My life is changed because I value staying connected to my church community. I am blessed and I am a blessing when I stay connected.

NOTES

THANKFUL

REJOICE ALWAYS; pray continually; give thanks in all circumstances, for this is God's will for you in Christ Jesus. (1 Thessalonians 5:16-18 NIV)

It is super hard to maintain a posture of thankfulness when your kids are fighting, the house is a mess, dinner's waiting to be made, and the to do list goes on and on into the next day. Granted, everyone's list of responsibilities looks different, but the feelings are close to the same. Yet, we see a clear reminder to, "Be joyful always; pray continually; give thanks in ALL circumstances."

How does one maintain a posture of thankfulness in the midst of living this life with its challenges, highs, lows, and everything in between? We CHOOSE to be thankful! Is it easy? Sometimes, YES… a lot of the times, NO. A choice is being made every day we wake up of whether we are going to partner with the Holy Spirit to help us. We CHOOSE. It's all about changing the way we think and the perspective in which we see things.

If I approach each day with a heart of thankfulness to my Creator, He will show me the numerous things for which I can be thankful. When I struggle, He reminds me to, "pray continually," because prayer works!

DECLARE: I CHOOSE to be thankful for this day. I choose to be thankful for this life I live and for those I share it. When I'm struggling, I won't grumble. Instead, I will pray. God hears me when I pray, and fills me with JOY in His presence. I am a thankful person; that's what people say about me!

NOTES

GROWTH

ANYONE WHO LIVES ON MILK, being still an infant is not acquainted with the teaching about righteousness. But solid food is for the mature, who by constant use have trained themselves to distinguish good from evil. (Hebrews 5:13-14 NIV)

A gift that was given to you when you accepted Jesus as your Savior, the gift of the Holy Spirit! What a tremendous gift to be given! I love that the Holy Spirit is always pushing us closer to God. The Holy Spirit will help us grow, if we ask Him. The Holy Spirit is not interested in us being content when it comes to the things of God! Hebrews chapter 5 verse 14 says, "...by constant use they trained themselves..." Growth is not occasional, it's continual, it's daily. Some days we have huge growth spurts (breakthroughs), other days we are simply faithful to do what He's asked us to do—we obey His word.

The problem in our society is that we want instant results, yet we know that anything worth having comes through discipline and hard work. Growth in life and more importantly growth God, requires CONSISTENCY. To whom much is given, much is required. If we cannot read God's word or seek him through worship or consistently pray for our families, then how can we grow? God is calling us higher.... now, let's do a happy dance!!!!

DECLARE: Today is the day that I start to consistently seek God through His word, worship, and prayer. I can do this. I want to do this. I accept the Holy Spirit's challenge to grow. Growing in God is going to be a fun adventure full of surprises!

NOTES

COURAGE

"...BE STRONG AND COURAGEOUS, for you must go with this people into the land that the Lord swore to their ancestors to give them, and you must divide it among them as their inheritance. The Lord himself goes before you and will be with you; he will never leave you nor forsake you. Do not be afraid; do not be discouraged." (Deuteronomy 31:7-8 NIV)

Courage is required in to live this life of faith. By faith we read and receive God's promises. By faith we take a dream and make it a reality. By faith we lay hands on the sick and they are healed. I believe faith and courage are best friends... courage is the wind beneath faith's wings! You better believe that faith and courage were working together in the Lion's Den with Daniel (Daniel chapter 6). Faith and courage were working together when David confronted Goliath. The Bible is full of faith and courage stories, take a look.

Pain, rejection, and loss are all things we experience as did Jesus. It's part of life. We take faith and walk it out, not knowing what the end will be. It takes courage to confront the pain, rejection, and loss and say, "I'm am stronger because of _____ (insert painful experience), because I walk by faith and exercise the courage to move forward in Christ. Courage does NOT stand still. Courage is an action. It is wrapped in love and found by those who are brave. I am thankful for the reminder to, "Be strong and courageous... because Jesus will never leave you or forsake you."

DECLARE: I will not be afraid of what the future holds. I pair my faith with courage, because I am brave. I have what it takes to confront pain, loss, and rejection... I have courage! I am thankful because I know that I am never forsaken and I am never alone, Jesus is my co-pilot.

NOTES

COMFORT

"HE HEALS THE BROKENHEARTED and binds up their wounds. Great is the Lord and mighty in power; his understanding has no limit." (Psalm 147:3, 5 NIV)

There are times in life that we experience such great loss that we feel we will be crushed under it. Sometimes it seems as if we move from one crises to another barely having time to come up for air. There are moments when we feel so alone and isolated that all we see is darkness. Tragedy changes people. No one fully knows what they can handle and what they are capable of walking through until they are forced to do so. We really are stronger than we think!

He heals the brokenhearted. We see it time and time again in Word of God. Let's look at Job… In Job chapter 17 we see the heart of a broken man, "My spirit is broken, my days are cut short, the grave awaits me… my days have passed, my plans are shattered, and so are the desires of my heart…." Job is utterly dismayed, a man who has lost (literally) everything. Yet we see God come like He promises. "But those who suffer He delivers in their suffering; he speaks to them in their affliction… He is wooing you from the jaws of distress to a place free from restriction." (Job 36) That's a good Father; full of mercy, compassion, and understanding. He offers comfort to those who trust Him and run into His open arms.

DECLARE: I reject the lie that I am alone in my sorrows, because I find comfort in the arms of Jesus. I reject the lie that I can't handle what comes my way, because I find comfort in the arms of Jesus. I am loved, I am comforted by Jesus.

NOTES

SELF-CONTROL

"BUT THE FRUIT OF THE SPIRIT is love, joy, peace, patience, kindness, goodness, faithfulness, gentleness and self control. Against such things there is no law. Those who belong to Christ Jesus have crucified the flesh with its passion and desires. Since we live by the Spirit, let us keep in step with the Spirit. Let us not become conceited, provoking and envying each other." (Galatians 5:22-26 NIV)

The constant reminder that we are to walk in self control at all times in every way for every situation is super easy, right? Wrong. Walking in self control when your "buttons" are deliberately being pushed is one of the hardest things to do. Dishonor me and I'm going to lay my self control down to set things straight. Disrespect my family and my self control grows wings and fly's away. When I'm tired and haven't had my coffee or my quiet time is interrupted, you'll soon find that my self control is still sleeping, just like I want to be—but I'm not and that's why my self control tank is half empty.

When I'm prayed up, coffee'd up, kids are cooperating, tasks are done - you'll find that I am the epitome of what self control looks like... And that's the problem, self control isn't developed in the semi perfect moments of bliss. Self control is developed in the trenches of hard life. It is developed when life is messy and we don't feel like doing the right thing, but we do it anyways because we have the best cheerleader ever, the Holy Spirit! I believe that we have more self control than we recognize. Remember, you're not alone on this journey, the Holy Spirit will help you, that's what He does.

DECLARE: I walk in the fruit of the Spirit because I have the Holy Spirit in me. When it's hard, I have self control. Yes, I have self control.

NOTES

TRUST

".... DO NOT WORRY about what to say or how to say it. At that time you will be given what to say, for it will not be you speaking, but he Spirit of your Father speaking through you." (Matthew 10:19-20 NIV)

Trust is a choice. We choose if we are going to trust God, family, and friends. There are times when those closest to us can hurt us, betray us, or make us feel less than who we are... but never God... God is an ever present help - always! In the specific situations that we trusted people and they let us down, it's important to remember that God will give us both the words and the timing of what needs to be said. Timing is everything with God, and it needs to be the same for us... waiting on God, trusting God, because He is always faithful. I don't need to worry or fear about confrontational or difficult conversations. Please understand, in these moments it's not what we feel like saying, it's what God is saying... which is often different than what we're feeling! During these times, we are presented with an opportunity to grow, and we growing is important.

We read in 1 Samuel chapter 3 that the Lord was with Samuel as he grew up, and he let none of his words fall to the ground... The Lord revealed himself to Samuel through his Word (1 Samuel 3:18 - 21). God trusted Samuel to say what needed to be said when it needed to be said. We can do the same, we can release the words God gives us to bring change to our city and world for the Glory of God!

DECLARE: I will not be afraid of what to say, because I trust God to give me the right words. The words I speak bring healing and restoration. I know God's voice, and I obey Him.

NOTES

TRIALS

"CONSIDER IT PURE JOY, my brothers, whenever you face trials of many kinds, because you know that the testing of your faith produces perseverance. Let Perseverance finish its work so that you may be mature and complete, not lacking anything." (James 1:2-4 NIV)

Rejoice in the trial, again I say rejoice... how can that be? How can we possibly find joy when we face trials? Trials are hard, they're tiresome. Trials aren't fun, but they are necessary if we really want to grow. Unfortunately in todays day and age, there is a 'something for nothing' mentality floating around and it's causing a lot of damage in peoples' lives. Many want to take the easy road and get the results of those that took the tough road and fought the good fight of faith. Those that persevere through their trials place a greater value on their breakthrough and growth, and they're not to eager to lay it down for the easy way. When your faith is tested, it's because you can handle it! Trials will come, don't be afraid of them.

I believe we are all called to lead in some capacity. A leaders should face trials and says, "How can I grow through this trial?," "What can I learn through this trial?" It's super important when walking through a trial NOT to play the "blame game," that only stunts our growth and causes us to stop growing. God doesn't want us to lack anything while we're here on the earth, He's teaching us about ourselves when we walk through trials. It should bring us JOY to know that trials don't last and we're not alone in them. If we obey, if we trust, we will always win.

DECLARE: I walk with JOY through trials because I am not alone. Trials help me grow, I want to grow. I am complete, in Christ, lacking nothing. This truth fills me with great HOPE.

NOTES

FREEDOM

"YOU, MY BROTHERS AND SISTERS, were called to be free. But do not use your freedom to indulge the flesh; rather, serve one another humbly in love." (Galatians 5:13)

I believe that we grow in our understanding of what true freedom is when we learn to love others well. You can't be truly free if you don't love. It starts by loving what God created in YOU. You must be able to love yourself before you can truly love others. That's where the enemy gets us. He gets us to focus on all our flaws or weaknesses, then we tear other people down to make ourselves feel better in a ruthless cycle of destruction to ourselves and potential healthy relationships with others. As the word says in Luke chapter 12:3, "...what you have whispered in the ear in the inner rooms will be proclaimed from the roofs." It's only a matter of time before your deep inner beliefs spill out of you. So many walk around proclaiming to be free, but don't love others. The fruit of freedom is LOVE.

I'm so thankful God sent the Holy Spirit to help us. We need help—everyday we need help and that's OK! When we try to love people without the help of the Holy Spirit, we find ourselves loving inconsistently and needing a lot more alone time—away from people. However, with the Holy Spirit's help, we are drawn to people and find loving them doable and actually quite pleasant. We can love ourselves and people well everyday. Let's thank Holy Spirit.

DECLARE: I love who I am, and I love who God created me to be! I walk in freedom because I walk in love. I love people well because the Holy Spirit helps me.

NOTES

PEACE

"THE LORD GIVES STRENGTH to his people; the Lord blesses his people with peace. I will listen to what God the Lord says; He promises peace to his people, his faithful servants—but let them not return to folly." (Psalms 29:11, 85:8 NIV)

We love those moments in life that are full of peace, beautiful peace, we crave these moments, we cling to these moments. Then, life comes at us with all its messy chaos, and we lay down our peace to tend to the messes and chaos. Our stress rises, our smile fades and suddenly we are Miss Grumpy Pants! It takes intentional discipline to hold on to our peace when life gets messy.

We read in Luke 10 about a person at peace with their choices. Mary sat at the Lord's feet listening to what he said. But Martha was distracted by all the preparations that had to be made... The Lord responds, saying, "You are worried and upset about many things (Martha), but only one thing is needed. Mary has chosen what is better..." (Luke 10:38-41) God wants us to choose what is better, He wants us to choose peace. The beautiful thing about choosing peace is that it is always available to us as daughters of a loving heavenly Father.

I believe the challenge is to grow in the areas that continually steal our peace. As Psalms 85 says, "do not return to folly." Learn from the mistakes that steal your peace, and put a stop to it. The Holy Spirit is there to help. We can hold onto our peace.

DECLARE: With the help of the Holy Spirit, I will keep my peace. When I allow things to steal my peace, I will quickly repent and be restored. I can walk in peace in every situation I face, I believe this.

NOTES

JOY

I SAY TO THE LORD, "You are my Lord; apart from you I have no good thing. You make known to me the path of life; you will fill me with joy in your presence, with eternal pleasures at you right hand." (Psalms 16:2, 11 NIV)

Picture the perfect family vacation; disconnected from technology and connected with those you love the most. You're enjoying the food, the conversations, the adventures, and all the joyful up until the last day before you have to go back to "normal" life. The to do list you start creating in your head is a mile long and then the moment arrives when the recent JOY of beautiful sunny beaches slips away and you are left packing for home anticipating post trip laundry duty.

Life shouldn't feel this way, but a lot of the time it does! We're just holding on until the next "fun" thing to get our jolt of JOY! "If I can just make it to Friday," we say, "I can have a break from the stress, and go to the movies (or dinner, or bowling, or whatever is fun to you)." I BELIEVE we can live in JOY versus getting periodic jolts of JOY, I really do!

Abiding in God's presence is the KEY to living in JOY. The older I get the more I realize how easy it is to abide in His presence. The pressure to perform decreases and my desire for Him increases... until no matter what I'm doing—I'm abiding in Him and He with me. Talking to Jesus all day long about every detail connects me to His heart, God cares about the details of my life and my days.

DECLARE: I am filled with JOY in God's presence, I love to talk to Him and share my heart with Him. I will not strive for Joy, I will walk in JOY because I have the Holy Spirit in me—and He's helping me! I have JOY!

NOTES

RESTLESS

"IN MY DREAM I saw seven heads of grain, full and good, growing on a single stalk. After them, seven other heads sprouted—withered and thin and scorched by the east wind. The thin heads of grain swallowed up the seven good heads. I told this to the magicians, but none of them could explain it to me." (Genesis 41:22-24 NIV)

Have you ever entered a season in your life when you felt bored and restless? Are there days that seem to drag on with no end it sight? The monotony of the next day looking the same makes you want to run away and find adventure? Be encouraged in the fact that you are not alone in feeling this way, many get stuck in a rut and become restless about what their future holds.

Look at Pharaoh in Genesis 41, He's having dreams and begging someone to tell him what they mean. He's restless about unknown interpretation of what they mean. The key here is, He didn't give up! Pharaoh kept looking until he found his answer and his breakthrough. Here is a valuable lesson. When we are confronted with restlessness, we MUST choose to press on until we breakthrough. We can find joy in the mundane by talking to the Holy Spirit and asking Him to highlight what He's doing in those moments.

Restlessness is a trap the enemy sets hoping we will believe lies. I challenge you to see God in the details of your day. Use the time to pray to a God who hears and responds while completing chores. When you become restless and frustrated with 'more of the same,' I challenge you to see how God is developing you and shaping you into His image and likeness. What you're doing, no matter how big or small is important — place a value on what you do!

DECLARE: When I am tempted with restlessness, I will respond with prayer and a attitude of thankfulness. I will confront each task I must do with joy, excellence, and a good attitude. I trust that God is doing a work in me that will produce lasting fruit. I am faithful.

NOTES

DISCIPLE

"AND WHOEVER DOES NOT CARRY their cross and follow me cannot be my disciple. In the same way, those of you who do not give up everything you have cannot be my disciples." (Luke 14:27, 33 NIV)

In a world where most people want something for nothing, and laziness is increasingly tolerated, carrying one's cross does not sound that appealing. Doing the hard work to get the results we crave can seem impossible and out of reach. Yet, the Spirit on the inside of us continually challenges us to push through to conquer our fears and failures. The result is growing stronger and becoming more like our Creator! But—why does it have to be so hard? Because, we were created to do hard things and win, that's our DNA—we're winners, not quitters!

The problem is, we're letting the wrong people talk into our ears and tell us what we can't do, and we believe them. What about THE CHAMPION FIGHTER living on the inside of us who believes in who we are? Why don't we give His voice the same recognition we give to the voice of the doubter? The answer is, it's easier to quit than it is to fight - but we hate the feeling of quitting, because it's not in our DNA to quit!

Jesus says in Luke 14 that we have to give up everything to be His disciple. This includes our fear of failure, our insecurities, control, anger, and needing the voice of others above His. The list can go on and on. We have to give up EVERYTHING to be His disciple, only to discover the cost cannot begin to compare to the riches of being a disciple of Jesus. The love, joy, peace, patience, goodness, kindness, gentleness, faithfulness, and self-control that we receive and give will always be worth the cost of being His disciple.

DECLARE: I will not shrink back in my responsibilities as a disciple of Jesus Christ. I am not afraid of what is required of me, and I trust that I have what is needed to do my job well. I embrace the call of God on my life and count it an honor to serve my Savior all the days of my life. Thank you, Holy Spirit, for helping me every step of the ways.

NOTES

SELFLESS

"FOR CHRIST'S LOVE COMPELS US, because we are convinced that one died for all, and therefore all died. And he died for all, that those who live should no longer live for themselves but for him who died for them and was raised again. So from now on we regard no one from a worldly point of view... if anyone is in Christ, the new creation has come: The old has gone, the new is here!" (2 Corinthians 5: 14-17 NIV)

We are all part of a family in some sort or another. For some it's a good thing and for others, it's a difficult thing. There are those whose mothers and fathers never demonstrated what it was to be selfless. Some of us were abandoned and some of us were orphaned. Some of us had parents that were the epitome of selflessness, always putting others needs before themselves. Regardless of your family dynamic, Christ has led us by His example of love and selflessness, and we are commanded to follow HIS ways not our own.

I'm often reminded throughout my day that Jesus was tempted and tested in every way that I am and more! God is calling me higher, He's calling YOU higher—and the only way we can go higher is to become selfless. Becoming selfless is dying to what self wants, what self thinks it needs, and what self does and doesn't do. Dying to self is becoming so God centered that selflessness is who we become without even trying. Yes, it is possible!

I'm excited to be on this journey, I'm excited to discover how great the Holy Spirit is on the inside of me, I'm excited to share with others the power and glory of God and to see them set free. I'm excited because I am never alone, I am never forsaken —I can do ALL things through Christ, because I am SELFLESS. God knows what I have need of, so I don't need to focus on such things, for they will surely be taken care of by a Father who see's and knows me.

DECLARE: It is not hard to be selfless, it is a choice I choose to make everyday. Selflessness brings me higher. I focus on all that God is doing NOW without a care or concern for my future, because God is in control. Yes, God is in control!

NOTES

DANCE

I WILL BUILD YOU UP AGAIN, and you will be rebuilt. Again you will take up your timbrels and go out to dance with the joyful. Then young women will dance and be glad, young men and old as well. I will turn their mourning into gladness; I will give them comfort and joy instead of sorrow. (Jeremiah 31:4, 13 NIV)

Anyone of us can share times in our lives when things turned out badly or we were hurt by someone we loved. All of us, at one time or another, have experienced loneliness or feelings of abandonment. These are not good feelings to have. We are left feeling less than we are! Sadly, there will be moments in our future when these same feelings present themselves and we will have to choose whether or not we partner with them. We and we alone have the power to choose what we will allow.

I believe God wants to teach us how to dance upon the feet of injustice. Not to say that there won't be moments when we mourn loss or face trauma, but we don't LIVE in those places. We travel through them to promised greener pastures. God's destiny for us is full of good things, things we can't make happen for ourselves… things so good, in fact, they make us want to DANCE for JOY.

In Jeremiah 31, we can see that God is preparing the Israelites for a difficult time in their lives with a promise of better things following. He tells them that they will be rebuilt and they will dance again. The frustration for people is that they stall in the middle of the battle and think God has forsaken them. Yet, He promised, "Never will I leave you or forsake you."

DECLARE: I will not stall in the battle, I will persevere and have a dance party at the end of every victory. God is for me, He will sustain me and give me the strength I need to get to my dance party. I believe there are a lot of dance parties in my future!

NOTES

GENEROUS

"I WAS YOUNG AND NOW I AM OLD, yet I have never seen the righteous forsaken or their children begging bread. They are always generous and lend freely; their children will be a blessing. Turn from evil and do good; then you will dwell in the land forever. For the Lord loves the just and will not forsake his faithful ones." (Psalm 37:25-28 NIV)

I love the Bible and the simple truths found in it. One of the resounding theme's found in Scripture is generosity. Jesus led by example when in came to generosity, He was extremely generous when it came to His time, teaching, and ministry. You can see throughout the New Testament how much He loved people, His level of compassion blows my mind every time I read the gospels. Jesus was generosity personified, and we should be too!

In Psalms 37, we get a glimpse into David's life. We get a picture of what he lived through on his journey to eternity. He battled as a military leader; was endlessly pursued and forces wanted to kill him. His was not an easy life—but a blessed one. David describes the righteous, and the fruit that comes from it. Many aspire to live the blessed life of the generous without the time and investment required. Generosity is a lifestyle and the by-product is being blessed in every way. According to David, "I've never seen the righteous forsaken or their seed begging bread." The needs of the generous are met first and consistently by their own generosity to others.

The mindset of a generous person is, "All I have belongs to the Lord, and I am a steward of the blessings given to me; therefore, I will faithfully sow seed into the ground for the sake of the Kingdom." As they sow in generosity, they reap a harvest of provision in every area of their life. There is no fear of lack in the life of a generous person. I love the joy attached to the life of a generous person. They exude a life filled with joy because of what they live.

DECLARE: I choose to be a generous person. I make my time with the Lord a priority so what I get from Him I can give away. I believe I am blessed to be a blessing. I am learning to be content in all things.

NOTES

FEAR

"EVEN THOUGH I WALK through the darkest valley, I will fear no evil, for you are with me; your rod and your staff, they comfort me. The LORD is my light and my salvation—whom shall I fear? The LORD is the stronghold of my life—of whom shall I be afraid? The LORD is with me; I will not be afraid." (Psalms 23:4, 27:1, 118:6 NIV)

When we take our eye's off of the prize and become detoured by distractions, it's easy for fear to creep trying to suffocate us! The thing about suffocation is that it doesn't happen without us knowing it. We can't pretend we're not suffocating because we'll die. We need oxygen, it is life. It's the same thing with our connection to Father; without it we will die.

Many of us battle fear on a daily basis! I've met many that conquer fear and live at peace most of the time, but not all of the time. Do I believe it is possible? I sure do.

Learning to live from a place of peace, regardless of our surrounding conditions, comes from living a life of surrender. Surrender is giving up the need and desire to be right. Surrender is giving up the need to control others and circumstances. Surrender is a selfless act that involves walking in LOVE no matter what—towards anyone. I'm glad surrender is easy (insert hearty laugh)! I cling to Philippians 4:13: I can do ALL things through Christ who gives me strength. It is a lifeline that anchors me when bad things happen. It shows me how to live a FEARLESS life! Everyday I spend here on this beautiful earth, I accept the challenge to embrace what comes with a posture of peace because I believe God is in control.

DECLARE: When fear comes to knock at my door, I do not open it! When thought's of fear pop up, I resist them and they have to go. I declare I am a person full of God's peace, and I am eager to share it with everyone I know. I AM a FEARLESS warrior that stomps on the lies of the enemy.

NOTES

LOVE

"LOVE THE LORD YOUR GOD with all your heart and with all your soul and with all your mind and with all your strength. Love your neighbor as yourself. There is no greater commandment greater than these." (Mark 12:30-31 NIV) Love must be sincere. Hate what is evil; cling to what is good." (Romans 12:9 NIV)

God is love. Apart from God we cannot love well—this includes ourselves and others! Our first priority is to Love God with all our heart, soul, mind, and strength... only when we do this FIRST are we able to walk in love towards others in the manner God expects! It demands our attention that the two greatest commandments are about LOVE; therefore, I believe we should invest every ounce of effort in understanding what this looks like and how to do it!

Love is a powerful force that heals. I'm sure that we can trace every broken relationship to the lack of love. Without the Holy Spirit to teach us what love looks like, we will be sporadic, inconsistent, and untrustworthy when in comes to relationships. In life, we need relationships. We need connections with people. Needing people is a good thing. However, if you've been hurt and remained unhealed, you can view needing people as a weakness.

By sending His only Son, God paints the perfect picture of what comprises real LOVE. This is something I don't know we will ever fully comprehend until we meet Him one day. We can't allow this incomplete understanding to stop us from pursuing God's love for us and letting His love in us create happy, healthy relationships. God is love and His love is perfect — how about we pursue His perfect love and trust that He will teach us how to manage and release it to those we are around?

DECLARE: God's love is in me and it helps me every day in every situation. As I keep my love on, God's love is poured out and I change lives. I love God, others, and myself well.

NOTES

POWER

"HE SAID TO THEM: "It is not for you to know the times or dates the Father has set by his own authority. But you will receive power when the Holy Spirit comes on you; and you will be my witnesses in Jerusalem, and in all Judea and Samaria, and to the ends of the earth." (Acts 1:7-8 NIV)

The Holy Spirit comes IN power and WITH power. He is aware of what we need. Each day is full of unexpected pleasures and frustrations. Life is unpredictable and glorious at the same time. When we divert our eyes from the truth that we are not alone and don't have to do it alone we become powerless NOT powerful.

Jesus said we would receive power when the Holy Spirit comes on us. We have to invite the Holy Spirit to come, and we have to make room for Him to live and abide when He comes. Many times we extend social invitations without making preparations, only to find we're not ready or prepared for our guest(s). So we spend our time scurrying and rushing around therefore missing the purpose of inviting people over—which is, to fellowship! When we invite the Holy Spirit to come, He wants to come and He wants to fellowship with us.

To walk in the level to which we're called, we need to change into the likeness of our Creator. The Bible says we are made in His image! In order to change the world around us, we need to press into what the Holy Spirit is saying and doing in us and around us. He created us for so much more! Yes, there are those who are lost and disconnected from this reality. This is why He is gives us the power to present Jesus to a lost and dying world. The power on the inside of you can save a soul from hell. The power given to us is ALL for the glory of God.

DECLARE: I believe the power of the Holy Spirit is in me and on me to do greater works! I am a powerful person that changes the world around me. When I am tired or scared, I embrace the power of the Holy Spirit in me and I don't quit. I never quit.

NOTES

FUTURE

...CHOSEN BY GOD for this new life of love, dress in the wardrobe God picked out for you: compassion, kindness, humility, quiet strength, discipline. Be even-tempered, content with second place, quick to forgive an offense. Forgive as quickly and completely as the Master forgave you. And regardless of what else you put on, wear love. It's your basic, all-purpose garment. Never be without it. (Colossians 3:12-14 MSG)

Our future, should we choose, is full of God's best. God's best is beyond what we can imagine. We have to press into His presence, His Word, His truth in order to partake in all He has for us! We cannot lay hold of ALL that God has promised us if we neglect LOVE.

My two year old, Jonathan, is a free spirit—not one to be confined to clothing. He wants to feel the wind on his belly, legs, and toes. Often, at home, you will find him only in a diaper. As long as he's got on a diaper, he's good! Constrict him and he becomes the Hulk. It's that way with love. As long as you're clothed in love, your future is better than good, it's great. Constrict love and you find a destitute situation. Love needs wings. The wings are faith and partnered together, you have the recipe for success—now and for your future.

In order for my future to be full of God's power and presence I must be: full of compassion, kindness, humility, quiet strength, discipline, even-tempered, content, and quick to forgive. I know I'm walking in God's love when these traits are evident in all I do. With the help of the Holy Spirit, we can walk into our best future. The Holy Spirit will teach us how to think, act, and behave like a child of God. I truly believe the hand of God responds when I walk in faith that's powered by LOVE. I want God's best now into eternity and I'm not willing to sacrifice it for a lack of love. Love is the fuel to my faith.

DECLARE: I will not be afraid of what my future holds. I will walk in love even when it's hard, for the sake of my future. My future is full of answered prayers and favor. Heaven is my resource, and Jesus is my guide. I am excited about my future!

NOTES

REDEMPTION

IN HIM WE HAVE REDEMPTION through his blood, the forgiveness of sins, in accordance with the riches of God's grace. (Ephesians 1:7 NIV)

The definition of redemption is the action of saving or being saved from sin, error, or evil. A good understanding of redemption's meaning and application, should change the way we live life.

When my children make a mess and they don't want to clean it up, I don't withhold my love from them, but I do expect them to clean it up. Jesus had to come because we needed Him. We needed Him to show us the best life and how to live it. Learning from Jesus how to live our best life, requires that we understand that He expects us to clean up our messes too! Picture this scenario: God has bought me a beautiful car, I take it for a drive. I get it dirty. God wants me to clean my car. before I park it in the driveway. That's fair. Jesus owns a car wash, and tells me that I can use it free of charge when I need to. All I have to do is take my car to the car wash and clean it. I don't need to take my wallet because the bill has been paid. Why wouldn't I take advantage of this gift? Is it God's fault if I don't clean the car? Is it Jesus' fault if I don't drive to the car wash? No. The responsibility lies with me to make the right choice. I have to clean my car... my sin, my error. Jesus paid it all.

Redemption is God's beautiful plan for His creation, to be fully restored to a loving Father that loves us deeply. The enemy wants us to believe that God is standing with a stick waiting to beat us when we mess up. This is a lie. Our true repentance means redemption is complete in us. We are saved from sin and restored to the Father. Simple.

In order to partake in true redemption, we MUST walk in love and forgiveness towards everyone. This is possible or it wouldn't be required. The Holy Spirit is your helper.

DECLARE: I am redeemed. It is a gift to me and I receive it. I walk in love and forgiveness towards everyone and in so doing, I embrace this gift of redemption. Jesus paid it all so I could live a full, blessed life.

NOTES

RIGHTEOUSNESS

FOR THE WORD OF THE LORD is right and true; He is faithful in all he does. The Lord loves righteousness and justice; the earth is full of his unfailing love. (Psalms 33:4-5 NIV)

What is righteousness? It is the quality of being morally right. Doing the right thing at all times, no matter what. Righteousness is a by-product of obeying the two greatest commandment: 'Love the Lord your God with all your heart and with all your soul and with all your mind,' and 'Love your neighbor as yourself' (Matthew 22:37-38), When we obey these commandments, we become righteousness!!!

We are geniuses at making simple things complicated. It's simple, the Lord loves righteousness, so I love righteousness. Complicated says, "I can't love some people because they are unlovable"... "I can't forgive this offense because I'm justified." "I won't help because no one helps me." These very real, complicated scenario's happen EVERY day to us, and we have a choice to choose what's right or what makes us feel better. I'm not interested in feeling better, I'm only interested in what is RIGHT—which produces righteousness. Righteousness ultimately makes me a better person!

God made him who had no sin to be sin for us, so that in him we might become the righteousness of God (2 Corinthians 5:21). You have to accept that you are the righteousness of God, when you choose to live the two greatest commandments given—even when it hurts. Honestly, if it doesn't hurt, it's not worth it! Working out with my hubby every week at the gym hurts, but the results are worth it! It will always be worth it. Like Jacob and I always say to each other, "It's a lifestyle, not a fad." Righteousness is a lifestyle, not a feeling.

I become what I observe, listen to, study. What are you becoming? Do you like who you are?

DECLARE: I love God with all my heart, soul, and mind. I love my neighbor as myself. Even when it's hard, I love well. As I obey the two greatest commandments, I become righteousness. I am righteous.

NOTES

SLEEP

WHEN YOU LIE DOWN, you will not be afraid; when you lie down, your sleep will be sweet. (Proverbs 3:24 NIV)

I believe God wants us to sleep well and wake up rested and ready for the day ahead. I believe God will bless our sleep and give us heavenly dreams. I've talked to many people who don't sleep well, and I'm sad for them. I believe sleep deprivation is a real problem in our world today. I don't believe it is necessary to point the finger of blame at what causes it and what we need to stop doing to prevent it. I believe the answer it to speak about what helps us sleep well.

God is an ever present help in times of trouble (Psalms 46:1). Often times before we go to bed, we reminisce over the days events, and what tomorrow holds. I think this is a good thing to do. What becomes dangerous is not trusting that God is in control of today and tomorrow. God is into details. Sometimes we rush through the details of our day, and even rush into the details of the future bypassing what God is doing in the here and now. Can you here the chaos in what you just read? Who can sleep in chaos? Not me. I have to intentionally lay down my today and my tomorrow to Jesus EVERY SINGLE NIGHT. Only than do I sleep in perfect peace. This is good and this is normal.

When we depend on other things to provide for us what only God can provide, we invite counterfeit results into our lives. Counterfeits to God's best are short lived and temporary. Lay them down.

There are definitely times when God has come and interrupted my sleep with a call to rise and pray over a situation. However, any time my sleep has been interrupted by a heavenly assignment, God has sustained me the next day with the energy and sharpness I need. God is faithful.

DECLARE: I don't have trouble sleeping. I sleep in perfect peace, because my mind is fixed on the One who takes care of my EVERY need. I will not fear of what happened today or what might happen tomorrow. I sleep well and wake up rested and ready for the day ahead.

NOTES

DELIVERANCE

YOU ARE MY HIDING PLACE; you will protect me from trouble and surround me with songs of deliverance. (Psalms 32:7 NIV)

Most of us only sing when we're happy. Some of us don't sing at all. Some of us wish we could sing. Singing is a beautiful expression of our emotions in a moment when we are feeling good. Life is full of opportunities to sing, to cry, to shout, to be silent. On this journey to an eternity in heaven, we find ourselves in many situations that provide opportunities for us to sing, cry, shout… or be silent.

God is my compass. When life is good, bad, messy, or unfair —God is my compass. As we spend time in the Word and discover who God is, what He's done, and what He will do, we find that He is our deliverer in every situation—good or bad. The problem is that we will often put our compass in our pocket and take the wheel of life—trusting we know best. We rely on the fact that we have common sense and love God. We've become professionals on what works and what doesn't. We avoid what's uncomfortable and cling to what is familiar.

If God, my compass, is my safe place and the person I run to in times of trouble then why do I still fight for control in life's hard moments? Could it be that I don't trust He will deliver me? Do I shrink back at the thought of relinquishing full control into my Creator's perfect hands? Where is my level of trust that He will deliver me? The fact of life is this: We trust or we don't trust. Who do you trust?

I made a choice to trust a God who has promised to deliver me! My God, the Creator of the universe, has promised to deliver me. I believe this is true. The hope I have in a Deliverer that cannot fail, sustains me into eternity!

DECLARE: I put God first in my life. God is my deliverer. I don't have to be afraid of what comes my way, I will be delivered from every battle I fight. I will win every fight, because God is my deliverer! Thank you God, I love that I am not alone in the fight. I am a winner. I am delivered.

NOTES

PROSPERITY

BLESSED ARE ALL WHO FEAR THE LORD, who walk in obedience to him. You will eat the fruit of your labor; blessings and prosperity will be yours. (Psalms 128:1-2 NIV)

Cringe, here comes the prosperity message! Just kidding. Those believers in their faith and the Word of God know that we will be blessed here on the earth. God is good to His kids. That's a promise. We have a Father who has an unlimited supply to every resource we will ever need.

There are some simple guidelines to be observed and followed in order to participate in God's best for our lives. We've done an amazing job complicating God's commands. (I won't go there). Let's address the two greatest commandments: Love the Lord your God with all your heart, mind, soul, and strength; And love your neighbor as yourself. Follow these two commandments and you will prosper. Follow God's commands and you will prosper.

The dilemma is that many people interpret the two greatest commandments based on their personal limited understanding. Anyone who has a true understanding of God's Word, knows that there is no room for error in the two greatest commandments! It is these people who live a life of prosperity. Those who love God and others are the ones you will find prospering.

With this revelation, I have come to learn that my 'idea' of prosperity is not God's idea of prosperity. I'm more interested in experiencing God's idea of prosperity and I know you as well. God's idea of prosperity is eternal. It's complete and full of what we need now and in the future. It's learning to embrace the moment and being content in all things. It's bills paid; debts cancelled; and wisdom with finances. This is prosperity, becoming like Him while embracing the journey of who God is.

DECLARE: I am changing the way I view my finances, debts, and future. I am becoming like my heavenly Father. He is teaching me how to become like Him in every way. I am prosperous. I am blessed.

NOTES

PRAYER

THIS, THEN, IS HOW YOU SHOULD PRAY: 'Our Father in heaven, hallowed be your name, your kingdom come, your will be done, on earth as it is in heaven. Give us today our daily bread. And forgive us our debts, as we also have forgiven our debtors. And lead us not into temptation, but deliver us from the evil one.' (Matthew 6:9-13 NIV)

I will be so bold as to say, "If you don't pray, you will ultimately fail." Success is based on an eternity spent in Heaven with our Creator. Yes, there are those that 'have it all,' according to society's standards, but their eternal wealth is found in hell. This is harsh, I know. We can read throughout the gospels how Jesus would go to a solitary place to pray. Jesus put an emphasis on prayer. If Jesus needed to pray, how much more do we need to pray?

I love that Jesus didn't hide from us how to pray. Jesus, who lived a life of prayer and communication with God, taught us how to pray. The Bible is full of prayers. If the Bible is full of prayers, prayer is important! Everyone who did anything significant for God can be found praying to Him. God responds to prayers prayed in faith. THIS is the key: faith. I cannot pray in doubt and think that I have God's attention. God is fueled by my prayers of FAITH.

While I was pregnant with Jonathan, we almost lost him and I almost when into complete liver failure. It was a dark moment for everyone. The doctors; test results; my body were all indicating bad things were happening and the end result could be worse. In this critical time our prayers of faith rose up against what EVERYTHING and EVERYONE was saying to declare the promises of God over ourselves and our baby boy. Do you believe when you pray that God will move? The results speak for themselves. We rose up through the pain, the torment, the tests, and declared life over Jonathan and over me—and that's just what we got, LIFE! I believe God answered our prayers of faith!!! I live it everyday.

DECLARE: I have faith when I pray. God responds to my prayers of faith. I will pray over everything I am facing and trust that God will answer.

NOTES

VOICE

GOD CALLED AGAIN, "SAMUEL!"—the third time! Yet again Samuel got up and went to Eli, "Yes? I heard you call me. Here I am." That's when it dawned on Eli that God was calling the boy. So Eli directed Samuel, "Go back and lie down. If the voice calls again, say, 'Speak, God. I'm your servant, ready to listen.'" Samuel returned to his bed. (1 Samuel 3:8-9 NIV)

Here I am. I am listening. My heart is ready. I am willing. So many feel this way about responding to God's call. The challenge lies within the many voices that are competing for our attention and for our time. We begin to question if we really know how to hear God's voice!

Look at Samuel. He knew he heard a voice calling his name, and he assumed it was Eli. Thankfully, Eli knew what was happening (after the third time). He tells Samuel, "Go back and lie down and if the voice calls again, say, 'Speak, God. I'm your servant, ready to listen.'" Samuel could hear, he was just confused about who was speaking.

This reminds me of the times I've taken my children to the park, and tons of kids are running and playing. I can become anxious when there are so many faces and voices and I lose sight of my own children in the maze of moving bodies. However, when my child call's my name, I know my child's voice and I respond. It doesn't matter where they are, I know their voice and I follow it to their face.

God's voice is always leading us to His face. He loves us, He call's us by name. What we need to do is ask the Holy Spirit what voices we have allowed to drown out the voice of God? What voices have we allowed to speak into our lives that go against God's promises? Please realize that we have a voice too! We can cancel and reject any lie that contradicts God's promises. We must use our voices too!

DECLARE: I know God's voice, I hear God's voice, and I respond to God's voice. I trust the Holy Spirit to highlight the wrong voices speaking into my life, and I repent for putting them above God's voice. I am forgiven and I am growing!

NOTES

SHAME

INSTEAD OF YOUR SHAME you will receive a double portion, and instead of disgrace you will rejoice in your inheritance. And so you will inherit a double portion in your land, and everlasting joy will be yours. (Isaiah 61:7)

I don't believe you can live in shame and walk in joy. I believe a person that is full of shame can have moments of happiness, but these moments will be temporary and short lived. Living in shame is like walking around with an alligator attached to your ankle—it hurts and it's noticeable. No matter how good you are at planting a fake smile on your face or posting on Facebook how great your life is... the truth always comes out. You fight with shame leaks out. I ask, why? Why walk around carrying something that hurts and is noticeable? Jesus paid it all so you could be free from shame. You don't have to be ashamed. It's not God's plan for you.

Why do people carry shame? Does pride convince them that people will think less of them? Is there fear of being rejected? Are they believing a lie that they aren't fully forgiven? Have they not forgiven the one who abused them or neglected them or abandoned them? Perhaps they don't know how to lay it down? Regardless of the reason, it's not God's plan. God's plan is freedom and everlasting JOY!

There was a short season in my life where I turned to antidepressants instead of fully trusting God (I do believe there are those that require medicine while they walk out their healing and that is OK); however, God came to me and told me to lay them down and trust Him. I didn't and I felt shame for disobeying. So you know what I did? I obeyed God and the shame left and JOY came in its place. That's what God does when you give Him what's broken. He replaces it with something that will never break... His promises! It's SO important to obey what God say's, otherwise the enemy comes in like a flood to drown us in shame.

DECLARE: I will obey God no matter what. I will partner with Joy and reject shame. I will forgive, I will reject the pride of caring what people think and I will ask for help. God is with me and He will protect me!

NOTES

HONOR

WEALTH AND HONOR come from you; you are the ruler of all things. In your hands are strength and power to exalt and give strength to all. Now, our God, we give you thanks, and praise your glorious name. (1 Chronicles: 29:12-13)

Honor—it's a hot topic right now. There are so many viewpoints on what honor is and what it looks like. Some are good and some are horribly wrong! I'm so thankful for a God that helps us fully understand what honor is and how to walk in it. When I'm not sure, God is. I am reminded in 1 Chronicles 29, that honor comes from God and He gives me strength to walk it out. So I WILL give Him thanks!!!

We all know it's super easy to honor others when there is no conflict or division. Introduce conflict and you will soon know if you are walking in honor even when it's hard. Honor isn't a feeling, it's a command. The second greatest command, "Love your neighbor as yourself" (Mark 12:33). To love others as we would love ourselves is to honor them. The Holy Spirit will help us grow in this area.

If you don't love yourself—for whatever reason—you will not be able to love others and therefore honor them. How do we continue to honor a person that is hateful? How do we honor a person that lies about us? Is it possible? Yes. It takes a person who loves themselves and values who they are. It is totally appropriate to establish safe boundaries and not allow others to verbally or physically abuse you and still maintain honor towards them. You are only responsible for how you behave and respond. You cannot control how others behave and respond. Lay down the need to control how people respond, and act towards you. Lay down your need to control situations and be yourself in every situation. Be free.

DECLARE: I love who I am and who God created me to be. I trust His plan for my life, it is a good plan. I choose to honor even when it's hard, because the Holy Spirit gently leads me and guides me into growing more like Jesus everyday. I honor well.

NOTES

CPSIA information can be obtained
at www.ICGtesting.com
Printed in the USA
LVOW04s0223301116
515072LV00015B/425/P

9 780692 748886